FOR ANNA METAXAS—E.M.

TO HIM AND SAVINIEN—R.P.

COPYRIGHT © 1992 RABBIT EARS PRODUCTIONS, INC., ROWAYTON, CONNECTICUT.
RABBIT EARS BOOKS IS AN IMPRINT OF RABBIT EARS PRODUCTIONS.
PUBLISHED BY PICTURE BOOK STUDIO LTD., SAXONVILLE, MASSACHUSETTS.
DISTRIBUTED IN THE UNITED STATES BY SIMON & SCHUSTER, NEW YORK, NEW YORK.
DISTRIBUTED IN CANADA BY VANWELL PUBLISHING, ST. CATHARINES, ONTARIO.
ALL RIGHTS RESERVED.
PRINTED IN HONG KONG.
1 2 3 4 5 6 7 8 9 10

LIBRARY OF CONGRESS CATALOGING IN PUBLICATION DATA
METAXAS, ERIC.
KING MIDAS AND THE GOLDEN TOUCH / WRITTEN BY ERIC METAXAS; ILLUSTRATED BY RODICA PRATO
P. CM.—(WE ALL HAVE TALES)
SUMMARY: A KING WHO WISHES FOR THE GOLDEN TOUCH IS FACED WITH ITS UNFORTUNATE CONSEQUENCES.
INCLUDES AN AUDIO CASSETTE WITH NARRATION AND MUSIC.
ISBN 0-88708-234-3 : $14.95. — ISBN 0-88708-235-1 : $19.95 (W/CASSETTE)
1. MIDAS—JUVENILE LITERATURE. [1. MIDAS. 2. MYTHOLOGY, GREEK.] I. PRATO, RODICA, ILL. II. TITLE. III. SERIES.
BL820.M55M48 1992
398.22—DC20   91-40670
CIP
AC

KING
MIDAS & THE
GOLDEN TOUCH

WRITTEN BY ERIC METAXAS

ILLUSTRATED BY RODICA PRATO

RABBIT EARS BOOKS

O nce upon a time, about twenty-seven centuries ago actually, somewhere on the coast of what is now Turkey, there was a sunny kingdom called Phrygia. And for many years the ruler of this kingdom was a certain King Midas. ✳ Now King Midas was a very wealthy man. Indeed, he had everything money could buy, but of all the things he possessed in the world, he valued nothing more than his only daughter. She was as dear to him as life itself, and it was for this very reason that he named her Zoe, which means life.

✳ Because the sun is very strong in Phrygia, most of the people who have ever lived there prefer to sleep during the afternoons and do their work during the cooler hours of the morning and evening. But it was precisely during those hot afternoon hours that King Midas' daughter loved to play most. And so dearly did the king love his daughter that he could not refuse her this wish.

So as his servants slept, he would contentedly sit and watch her play from the cool shade of his grape arbor, which overlooked his magnificent gardens, which, in turn, overlooked the brilliant blue sea. ✳ And during many of the long, sleepy afternoons in which he sat watching her run about chasing birds and smelling flowers, it was King Midas' particular habit to carefully count out some number of the gold coins that he possessed. ✳ There was quite a large number of them—in fact, he never could have counted them all—and each and every one of them, large and small, was exquisitely minted with the king's own regal profile. ✳ The likeness was perfect to the very tiniest detail, and had it not been for the small cosmetic addition of the six-rayed crown of the sun-

god Helios—with whom, in his heart of hearts, good King Midas liked to be identified—one might have easily mistaken the miniature golden image for the very king himself.

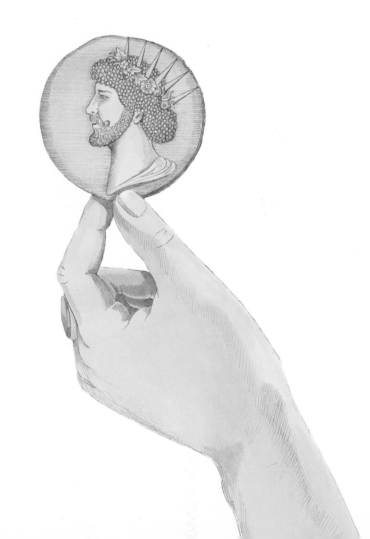

Now one day as he was sitting there in the arbor counting his coins, the king observed his daughter following a beautiful white butterfly as it flitted lazily down one of the garden paths. The butterfly was so marvelously delicate as to be almost transparent, and as King Midas watched it he could not help but admire the exceptional freedom and beauty of the creature. ✳ But as he beheld it, the strong rays of the Phrygian sun came to illuminate it in such a way that, for some time as it floated before him, it seemed to him to be made entirely of gold. ✳ The sight of this had the power of revelation and it so completely transfixed the king that long after the butterfly had flown out of his ken and on its way, he remained staring at where it had been as though under a powerful spell. ✳ And when he came to himself again, he remained consumed with the idea of it: *A butterfly made of gold! Astounding! I've never seen anything as beautiful in my life! I simply must have one! A butterfly made of gold!*

Now the idea of wanting a golden butterfly seemed at the time to be quite harmless. After all, he only wanted it to be able to give to his daughter. But as he ruminated further on the great beauty and worth of such an object, his small wish for a golden butterfly blossomed into an overwhelming desire that everything in the world might become gold. * *How beautiful the world would be if all things could be transformed as magnificently as the butterfly had,* he thought to himself. *If only I had the power to accomplish it. I should give anything to have that power— anything at all!*

* His obsession with this thought did not leave him for several weeks. But one day, when the wish became so fervent that he thought he couldn't stand it another moment, the king looked up and saw a golden chariot descending towards him out of the bright sun.

The curious being who debarked from it was dressed entirely in gold and claimed to be a messenger of none other than Helios the light-bearer himself. ✳ "Your most fervent wish has been heard, good King Midas," he said. ✳ "And it is our master's equally fervent wish that it should be granted. Therefore, as soon as the sun rises tomorrow you shall possess your desire—for as you will then perceive, all that you touch from that time forth shall turn to the purest gold!" ✳ Then, with a flourish of his hand, he conjured a brilliant box which he said contained a golden piece of the very sun itself. ✳ "A small gift for the good king!" he said. "For the good and great King Midas!" ✳ Naturally King Midas was deeply impressed, but when he reached out to touch the gift, it burned his hand. ✳ "Ah, yes," said the odd man with a queer smile. "Perhaps such a gift wasn't meant for your kind after all." ✳ With that he climbed back into his gilded chariot and again ascended into the blinding brilliance of the afternoon sun.

Of course all of this made the king quite eager for the next day. But when the sun's first rays entered his chamber in the morning, he became terribly uncomfortable. He tossed and turned endlessly about in his bed, but he was unable to find another moment's peace. And it was at some point soon thereafter that he came to realize that the very bed upon which he lay was made entirely of gold!

✳ Now, as you will doubtless understand, the king's joy at this realization can hardly be described. And the small price of a few hours of lost sleep was simply unworthy of comparing with the exquisite joy he now felt. Oh, he was elated! ✳ It next occurred to him that the odd messenger's promise must have come true and anything he touched might now turn to gold!

W ithout a moment's hesitation he was out of the bed and furiously looking about the room for a suitable object on which to experiment. He grew quite dizzy at the prospect of it all.

＊ At last his eyes came to rest on an ornately carved chair. He immediately moved toward it, and then, ever so cautiously, he touched it. Instantly it was transformed into a chair of the purest gold! On examining it more closely, King Midas saw that every part of it had been transformed—the upholstery, the carved wood—even the braided tassels that hung from it were gold! He could hardly believe his eyes. ＊ But the remarkable metamorphosis only seemed to whet his appetite for more. He saw a table just outside his bedchamber, and he touched it. He touched a tapestry! Then, as fast as his legs could carry him, he ran into the garden. He touched a marble statue! A vase! And everything he touched —every single thing—turned to gold! It was more than he could bear! ＊ Then King Midas stooped to pick up a white pebble. And no sooner had he touched it than it was gold! He saw another stone, slightly larger, and touched that and it too became gold!

The king next spotted a large conch shell that his daughter had discovered on the seashore. He remembered the day she had found it and recalled holding the shell to her ear so that she could hear the sounds of the ocean inside it, and how she had heard it saying, "thalassa, thalassa, thalassa," like the waves of the sea.

✳ In a flash he touched it, and it too was transformed to gold before his very eyes! It was magnificent! He lifted the golden conch to examine it and hold it to his ear, unable to imagine what golden music should come out of it now. But he found that it was extremely heavy, and when he held it up to his ear he heard absolutely nothing.

✳ Now, normally this would have saddened King Midas, but under the circumstances his thoughts turned rather quickly to the subject of what other objects he might turn to gold.

✳ In a moment his attention was captured by a beautiful flower. And when he touched it, the leaves, the stem, every petal, and even the intricate universe within the petals, turned to gold. He quickly touched another flower, and then another, and another! It was all too much to behold!

Then King Midas saw a white butterfly. It was quite like the one that he had so admired some weeks before, and as he was powerless to do anything else, he began to chase it. ✳ The chase took him down one garden path and then another until, as carefree as a small child, he completely lost track of himself. ✳ The butterfly eventually led him along the very edge of the castle parapet overlooking the ocean. And because the idea of having a golden butterfly consumed him so completely, he quite forgot about the long drop to the rocks below, and continued to chase it, teetering along the edge of the parapet as the butterfly danced just out of his reach. ✳ At last, reaching so far out that he nearly fell, the king succeeded in grazing the creature's gossamer wing with the tip of his outstretched index finger. But on the very instant that he did so, it stiffened to gold and fell away, out of his reach. Down, down it fell— all the way to the sea-washed rocks below, where it hit with a dull plink and disappeared among the barnacled crevices, a lifeless bauble. ✳ King Midas stood there staring at where it had fallen, unable to believe what he had just seen. He had never considered that he might kill the poor creature!

As he wound his way back to the palace King Midas passed several ancient olive trees and, tired from his chase, he leaned up against a particularly venerable specimen. ✳ As soon as he touched the trunk of the great tree, however, everything above him and around him froze into a single, golden moment. It was an extraordinary sight! The entire tree —its mammoth, gnarled trunk, every branch, every oval leaf, every green olive—had turned to gold.
✳ King Midas saw that even the hundreds of ants and other tiny insects on the tree had turned to gold. He beheld a golden inchworm, frozen in the act of measuring its last inch. There was a golden nest of golden eggs that would never hatch, and a golden hive of bees that would never produce honey again. Then, in a remote branch of the tree, he beheld the dazzling tracery of a golden spider's web—and finally, a long descending strand of golden spider's silk and the attached arachnid who had spun it, and would spin no more.

When he finally returned to the palace he called to his servants to prepare a banquet and cheerily announced to them that it would all be on plates of gold! Although they were quite puzzled, they complied with his request, and no sooner than they had set a plate before him did he touch it and turn it into gold before their eyes!

✳ Everyone was completely astounded, but King Midas only laughed and performed his magic on the silver goblet that was set before him. He then proceeded to turn all of the serving platters to gold as well as the very table on which they were placed.

✳ But when the novelty eroded and King Midas at last decided to get down to the actual business of eating, a curious thing happened. ✳ You see, when he picked up a fig to put into his mouth, it too turned to solid gold. And when he tried to pour himself a glass of wine, both the bottle as well as the liquid inside became gold! He then grew frantic, grabbing first a cluster of grapes and then a handful of olives. But to his great consternation, each and every thing that he touched turned quite indisputably into an object of solid gold! The king became deeply distressed. He would soon starve!

J ust then the king's daughter came running out of the palace to greet him. King Midas was so delighted to see her that he quickly embraced her. But no sooner did he do this than he recoiled in horror. For the golden touch with which he had been lately cursed had worked its hideous magic even on his precious daughter, whom he loved beyond anything in the world.

* "Oh, my Zoe!" he cried. "My dear Zoe, I have lost my dear Zoe!"

In his grief he began running, he knew not where.

✳ After a time, the king found himself at the edge of a stream. He sat down, exhausted, and putting his face in his hands, he began to sob. "I have lost my Zoe!" he cried. "I have killed everything that I have touched, and now I have killed the very thing in the world that was dearest to me. I don't wish to live! I don't care if I am the richest man in the universe!" ✳ But as he was crying the king noticed an odd thing. For somehow, the tears that were on his cheeks and in his hands hadn't turned to gold! Nor, inexplicably, had the stone upon which his hand rested! Was it possible? ✳ As fast as he could, King Midas ran back to the palace. With great trepidation, he touched one of the flowers that he had turned to gold. In an instant it became a living flower again! He touched another and another! *Oh, this is much too good to be true!* the king thought.

The king then ran to where his daughter stood. At the sight of her, tears came to his eyes again. Then, with a trembling hand, he touched her cheek. Immediately the warmth and color of life returned to her. The king immediately fell on his knees, and weeping with joy, he embraced the dear child tenderly. * "Oh, my Zoe, my Zoe!" he cried, "I have found my dear Zoe!" * And what the king said was quite true, for indeed, he had.

T hat day King Midas called a large feast. It was a celebration unlike anything the world had ever seen, even to this day. Every larder was emptied and nothing was spared—not a single thing—for you see, there was no earthly extravagance that could match King Midas' love for his daughter.

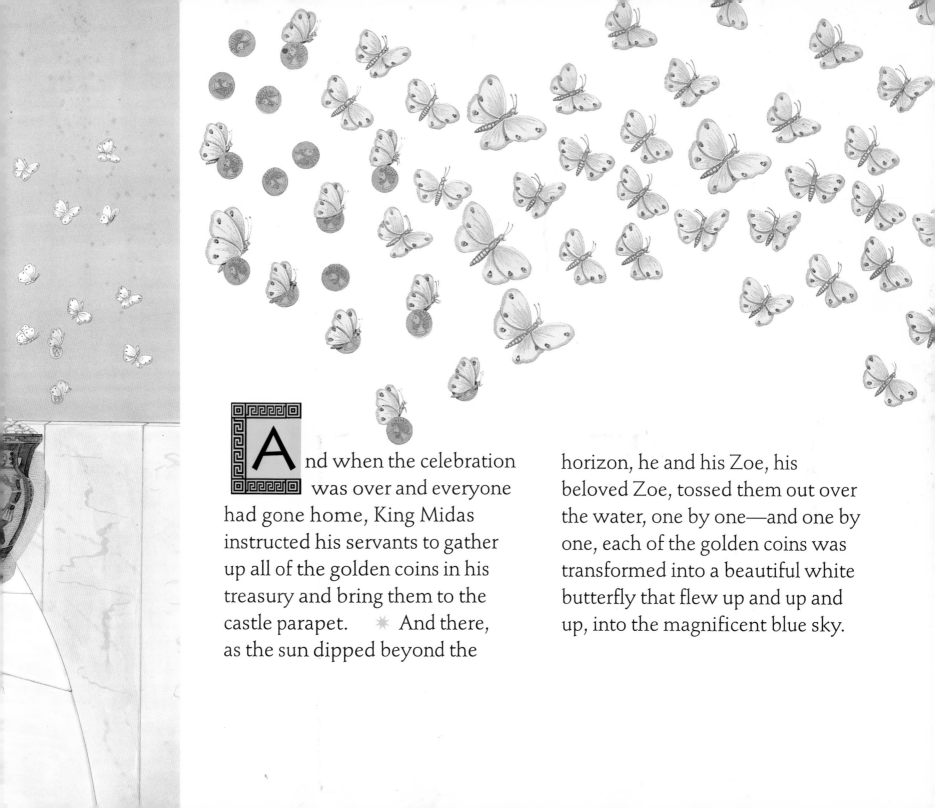

And when the celebration was over and everyone had gone home, King Midas instructed his servants to gather up all of the golden coins in his treasury and bring them to the castle parapet. ✳ And there, as the sun dipped beyond the horizon, he and his Zoe, his beloved Zoe, tossed them out over the water, one by one—and one by one, each of the golden coins was transformed into a beautiful white butterfly that flew up and up and up, into the magnificent blue sky.

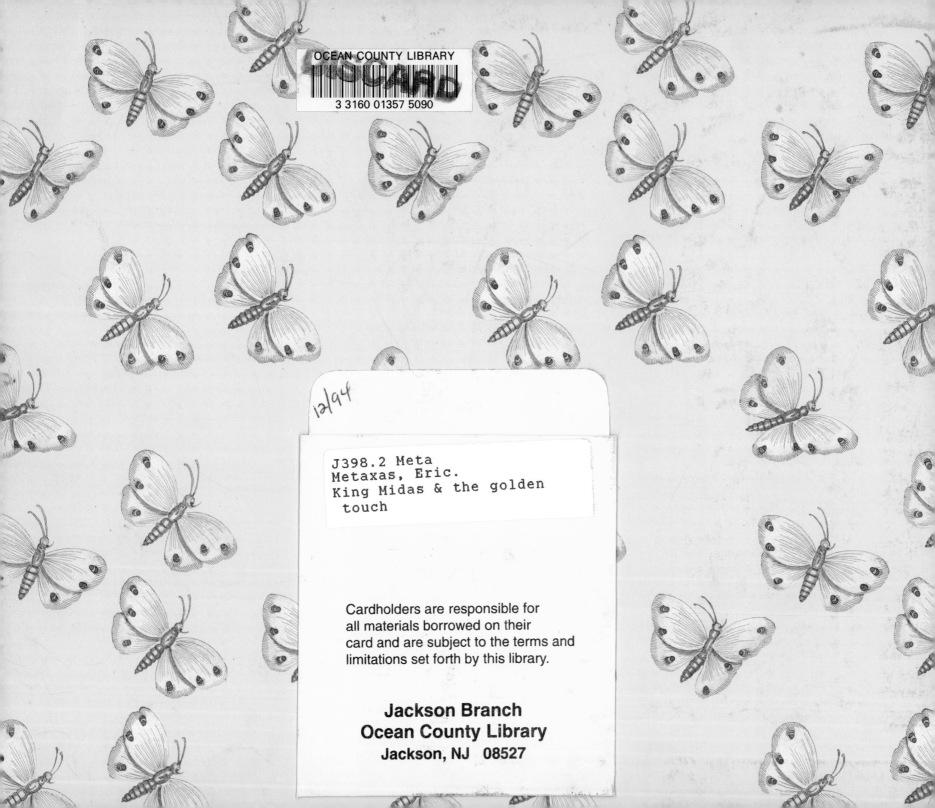